LIFE IN SPACE

David Glover

GW01043930

Heinemann Educational Publishers
Halley Court, Jordan Hill, Oxford OX2 8EJ
a division of Reed Educational & Professional Publishing Limited

Heinemann is a registered trademark of Reed Educational & Professional
Publishing Limited

OXFORD MELBOURNE AUCKLAND
JOHANNESBURG BLANTYRE GABORONE
IBADAN PORTSMOUTH(NH) USA CHICAGO

© David Glover, 1998
The moral right of the proprietor has been asserted.

First published 1998

02 01 00 99 98
10 9 8 7 6 5 4 3 2

British Library Cataloguing in Publication Data
A catalogue record for this book is available from the British Library.

ISBN 0 435 09659 1   *Life in Space* single copy

ISBN 0 435 09660 5   *Life in Space* 6 copy pack

All rights reserved. No part of this publication may be reproduced or transmitted
in any form, or by any means, electronic or mechanical, including photocopy,
recording or any information storage and retrieval system without permission in
writing from the publishers.

Illustrations
Julian Baker, title page, pages 8, 15, 19 and 23. Joe Lawrence, contents page and
page 21 bottom. Oxford Illustrators, pages 5 and 18. Arcana, page 11. Maltings
Partnership, page 21 top.

Photos
Photo Library International / Science Photo Library, page 5. Science Museum / Science
and Society Picture Library, page 6. NASA, pages 9, 10, 16 and 17 bottom. Genesis
Space Photo Library, pages 12 and 17 top. NASA / Science Pnoto Library, pages 13
and 20.

Designed by M2
Printed and bound in the UK

CONTENTS

WHAT IS SPACE?

On a dark night, when we look at the stars, we are looking into space. Space is the name we give to everything beyond our Earth.

What does space contain?

Space contains planets, stars, moons, meteors, asteroids, comets and many other objects. The whole of space and everything in it is called the universe.

The stars look like tiny dots of light in the night sky, but really they are much bigger than the Earth. They only look tiny because they are so far away.

The Sun – a special star

One star is much closer to the Earth than all the others. This is the Sun. The Sun is an ordinary star like billions of others in space. But the Sun is special to us, because it provides the heat and light that all living things on Earth need. The Earth travels around the Sun in a circle. We call this circle the Earth's **orbit**. The time the Earth takes to orbit the Sun is one year.

What is the Moon?

The Moon is a ball of rock which orbits the Earth. The Moon takes about one month for each of its orbits.

The Earth is not the only planet to have a moon. All the planets in the solar system, apart from Mercury and Venus, have their own moons.

Planet Earth is a huge ball made from solids such as rocks; liquids such as water; and gases such as air. The atmosphere is a layer of air that surrounds the Earth like a blanket. The atmosphere becomes thinner further away from the Earth. One hundred kilometres above the Earth's surface there is not enough air to breathe.

Earth is just one of nine planets that orbit the Sun. The Sun and its planets are called the solar system.

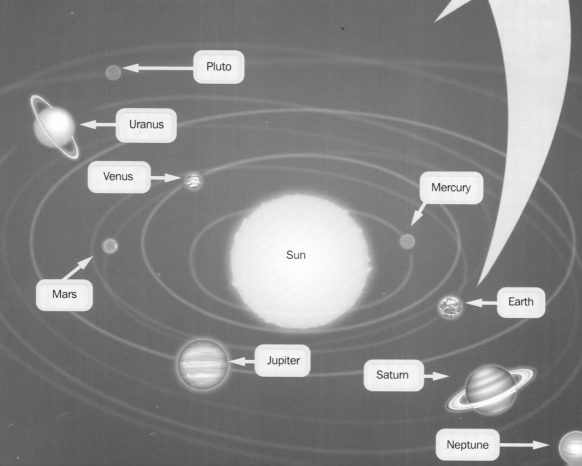

Pluto

Uranus

Venus

Mercury

Sun

Mars

Earth

Jupiter

Saturn

Neptune

WHY DO PEOPLE EXPLORE SPACE?

People have always wondered about the stars and planets. What are they made from? How far away are they? Can we travel to the stars? Space exploration has enabled us to find out much more about the universe.

Studying the sky

Most of what we know about the stars and planets has been discovered by **astronomers**. Astronomers are people who study the objects in space from Earth. They use telescopes to see how stars and planets move, and to measure their light. Astronomers have found that the distances to the planets and stars are fantastic. At the speed of a fast jet plane it would take 16 days to reach the Moon, 20 years to reach the Sun and half a million years to reach the next nearest star!

> **Italian scientist Galileo was the first astronomer to look at space through a telescope. He discovered that there are mountains on the Moon.**

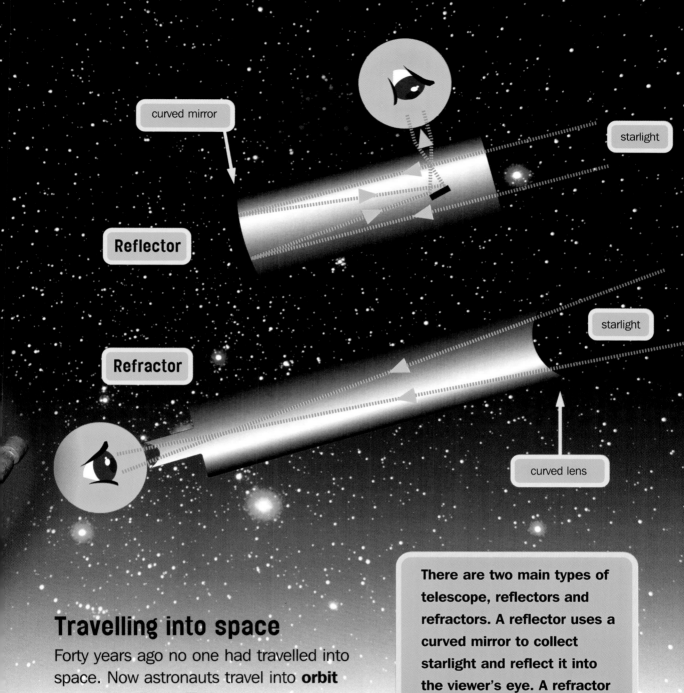

curved mirror

starlight

Reflector

Refractor

starlight

curved lens

Travelling into space

Forty years ago no one had travelled into space. Now astronauts travel into **orbit** around the Earth. They try out science experiments, repair **satellites** and test space travel equipment. The furthest that anyone has travelled from Earth is to the Moon and back. In future, as the Earth becomes more crowded, people may set out to live on the Moon and on other planets.

There are two main types of telescope, reflectors and refractors. A reflector uses a curved mirror to collect starlight and reflect it into the viewer's eye. A refractor uses a curved lens to gather the light and form an image.

HOW DOES A SPACECRAFT TAKE OFF AND LAND?

Astronauts travel into space inside spacecraft powered by **rockets**. The rocket engines burn fuel, which produces hot gases.

A Russian SL-4 rocket taking off. During take off, the astronauts are strapped into seats inside a capsule on top of the rocket. There is not much for them to do, as the take off is controlled by a computer.

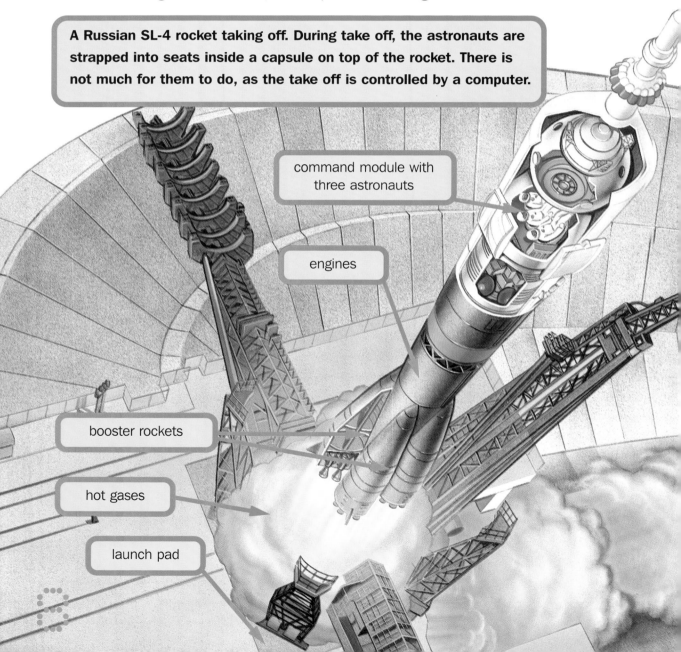

command module with three astronauts

engines

booster rockets

hot gases

launch pad

Taking off

When the spacecraft is ready to take off, the hot gases shoot out from the engines and push the rocket up from the ground. The force must be big enough to overcome the Earth's **gravity**. If you blow up a balloon, then let it go, it shoots off in the same kind of way.

The main rocket may be helped away from the **launch pad** by **booster rockets** fixed to its sides. When the rocket is going fast enough, the boosters fall away.

Staying in orbit

The rocket engines turn off when the spacecraft reaches **orbit**. It does not need engines to keep going in space because there is no air. This means that there is no **friction** so the spacecraft does not slow down.

Landing

When the astronauts want to return to Earth they turn on the engines to push their spacecraft out of orbit. Gravity then pulls the spacecraft back towards the Earth. The spacecraft may be slowed to a safe landing speed by parachutes. Many spacecraft splash down gently into the sea.

The space **shuttle** takes off from a launch pad like other rockets. But it has stubby wings so that it can land on a runway like an aeroplane.

HOW ARE ASTRONAUTS CHOSEN AND TRAINED?

Many people apply to be astronauts, but only a few are selected.
All astronauts studied science at school and college.

When astronauts are in **orbit** their bodies feel 'weightless'. They float around inside the spacecraft. Astronauts practise being weightless inside a special aeroplane, nicknamed the 'Vomit Comet'. The aeroplane dives towards the ground and the astronauts float around as if they were in orbit.

Space pilots and mission specialists

There are two types of astronaut: space pilots and mission specialists.

Space pilots fly spacecraft. Spacecraft are much faster and more complicated than the fastest aeroplanes, so new space pilots must already be jet pilots.

Mission specialists carry out science experiments or **satellite** repairs in space. Mission specialists must already be scientists or engineers before they apply to be astronauts.

What makes a good astronaut?

There is no age limit for astronauts. But when a **rocket** takes off, there is a tremendous force on the astronauts' bodies, so they must be fit and strong. New astronauts must prove that they can get along with each other without arguments, as they will be shut up together in a small spacecraft for weeks at a time.

This piece of equipment is like a fairground ride. It helps the astronauts to get used to spinning and turning at all angles, as they will during a space flight.

WHAT DO ASTRONAUTS DO IN SPACE?

The first astronauts went into space to prove that it was possible. Now astronauts have jobs to do. They launch new **satellites** and collect damaged satellites for repair. They carry out science experiments and build **space stations**.

Science in space

Space is a good place for science experiments because things are weightless. This means, for example, that chemicals do not settle into layers, so they can be mixed more evenly. It also means that astronauts can make special crystals for computer chips and very pure medicines that cannot be made so easily on Earth. In future, factories may be built on space stations to manufacture new materials and medicines.

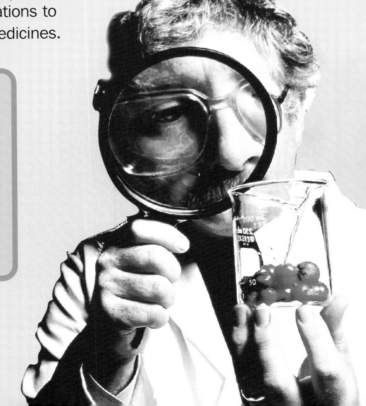

These tomatoes were grown on board a spacecraft. Astronauts do experiments to see how well plants grow when they are weightless. In the future, astronauts will need fresh food when they set out on long journeys to the planets.

WHY ARE SPACESUITS NECESSARY?

When they are inside the spacecraft, astronauts just wear ordinary clothes. But sometimes, like the astronaut on page 13, they need to go outside the spacecraft to carry out repairs or move loads around.

There is no air in space, so the **spacesuit** and helmet need to provide the astronaut with air to breathe. The air is kept clean and fresh by the life support system on the back of the spacesuit.

How does a spacesuit work?

A spacesuit is like a mini spacecraft. It is made from several layers of special cloth designed to protect the astronaut from specks of dust that may be travelling at thousands of miles per hour. It would be much too heavy to wear on Earth, but in space it is weightless.

Staying comfortable

Astronauts might easily get too hot inside their suits, so their underwear is water-cooled. The cooling water flows through plastic tubes.

The space helmet snaps onto a metal ring at the neck of the suit. It has a visor which the astronaut can lower to keep out bright sunlight.

Because there is no air in space there are no sounds. But the astronauts keep in touch with radios via a communications cap.

communications cap

helmet visor

thermal layer for warmth and protection

portable life support system

multi-layered spacesuit

jets of gas

This astronaut is wearing a spacesuit. He has a special backpack called an MMU (Manned Manoeuvring Unit). This squirts jets of gas to make the astronaut move up and down, forwards and backwards or left and right.

MMU hand controls

water-cooled underwear

15

HOW DO ASTRONAUTS LIVE IN SPACE?

Living in space can be tricky because everything is weightless, so special equipment is designed to overcome this problem. If astronauts tried to wash in a bowl, the water would just float away. If they lay down to sleep on an ordinary bed they might float up to the ceiling.

Space toilets

Going to the toilet is a special problem. There is no **gravity** to make liquids and solids drop into the toilet bowl. It could be very messy if the astronaut was not careful! Special space toilets have been invented to help. These work a bit like a vacuum cleaner. Suction draws the waste away. The suction is quite strong and astronauts sometimes get stuck to the seat. There are different shape seats for male and female astronauts.

Keeping fit

Because they are weightless, astronauts hardly use their muscles as they move around. They would soon lose their strength if they did not do exercises. Pedalling on exercise bikes helps them to keep fit.

SLEEP RESTRAINT

This astronaut is sleeping in a sleep station. She is strapped into a sleeping bag which holds her in place. Astronauts don't lie down to sleep in space because there is no down! They can fall asleep at any angle.

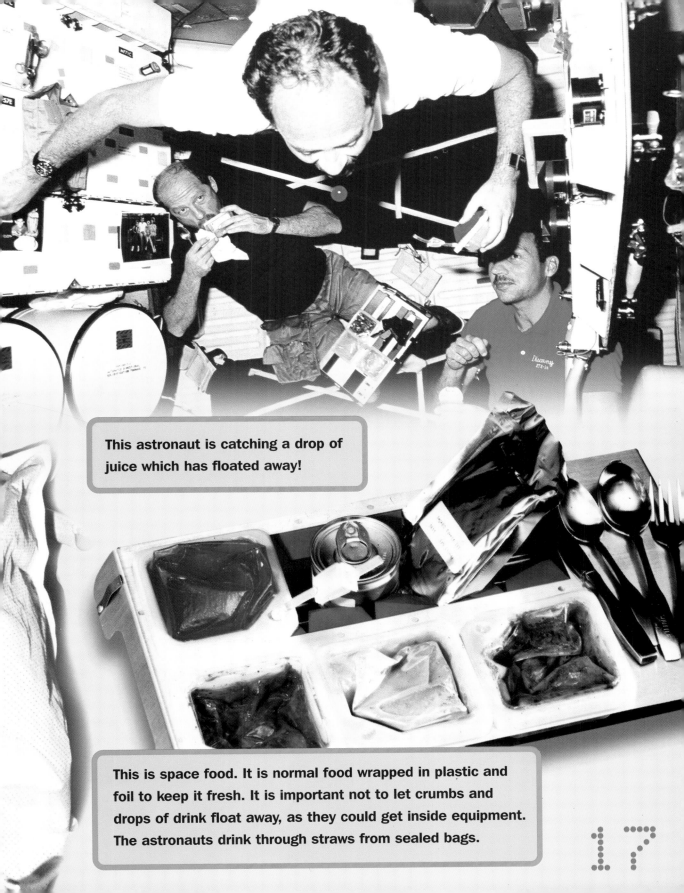

This astronaut is catching a drop of juice which has floated away!

This is space food. It is normal food wrapped in plastic and foil to keep it fresh. It is important not to let crumbs and drops of drink float away, as they could get inside equipment. The astronauts drink through straws from sealed bags.

17

HOW IS A SPACE STATION BUILT?

What is a space station?

A **space station** is like a house or an office that stays in **orbit**. Astronauts travel to space stations and live inside them, sometimes for months at a time. On board they carry out experiments in special laboratories, make observations and test equipment.

Constructing a space station

A space station is too big to be launched in one go by a **rocket**, so it is built up piece by piece from parts called modules. The modules are taken one at a time into space. They fit together like parts of a giant construction kit.

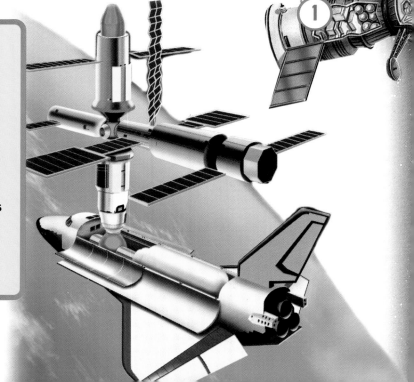

Modules are taken into space by a spacecraft such as the space **shuttle**. The modules have special round doors, called ports, which fasten together. Fixing one module to another is called **docking**. When two modules are docked the ports open, and astronauts can move between them.

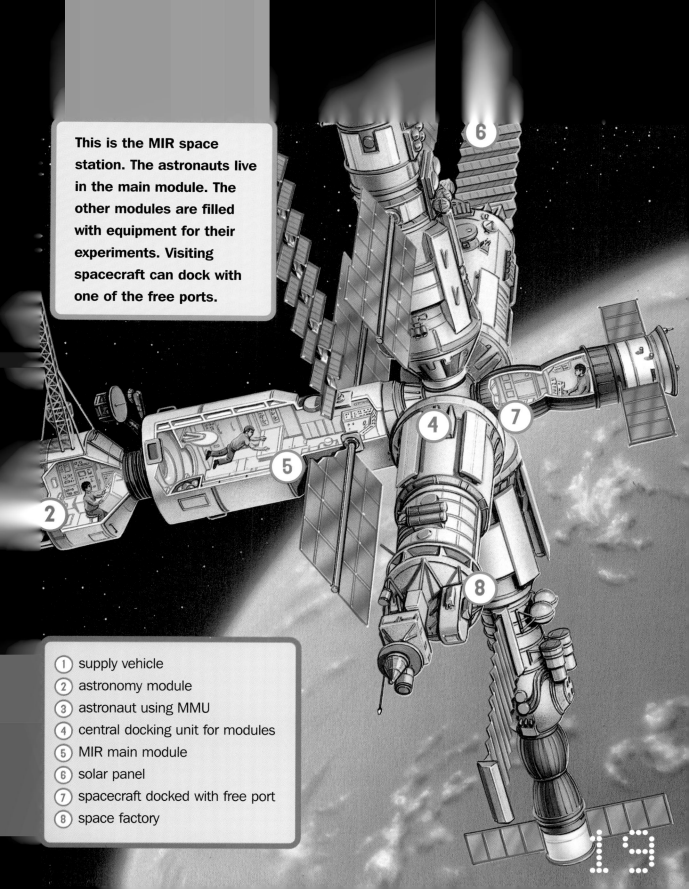

This is the MIR space station. The astronauts live in the main module. The other modules are filled with equipment for their experiments. Visiting spacecraft can dock with one of the free ports.

1. supply vehicle
2. astronomy module
3. astronaut using MMU
4. central docking unit for modules
5. MIR main module
6. solar panel
7. spacecraft docked with free port
8. space factory

WHAT DOES A SPACE PROBE DO?

A **space probe** is an unmanned spacecraft. Space probes take photographs, make measurements and beam their results back to scientists on Earth. Scientists use the information to learn what conditions are like on other planets.

How far can a space probe travel?

Space probes can travel much further than manned spacecraft. Robot space probes have been sent to most of the planets in the solar system. America and Russia have sent probes to explore Mars, Venus and Mercury. American probes have also been sent to the giant planets such as Jupiter.

Pathfinder was a 'lander' probe. It landed on Mars in 1997 using huge airbags to soften its landing. It released a rover vehicle called Sojourner. This picture shows the Pathfinder craft sitting on its deflated airbags. Sojourner, on the left, is analysing a rock.

Voyager was a 'fly-by' probe. In the 1980s it flew by Jupiter, Saturn, Uranus and Neptune and beamed back beautiful pictures. It has now travelled out of the solar system and is heading towards the stars.

The Mars observer was an 'orbiter' probe. In 1993 it was sent to **orbit** Mars and gather information. But it has broken down. Its signals are no longer being received on Earth.

Into the future

Space probes can help scientists to decide whether it is safe to send manned spacecraft to land on other planets. In 2011, America hopes to send a group of astronauts to Mars. Scientists also hope to set up a research station on the Moon. Perhaps in the future we might all be able to visit, or even live on, other planets!

SPACE TIMETABLE

	mission	purpose
1957	Sputnik 1	First satellite in orbit
1957	Sputnik 2	First animal in orbit (a dog called Laika)
1961	Vostok 1	First person in orbit (Yuri Gagarin)
1969	Apollo 11	First landing on the Moon
1973	Skylab	First space station
1976	Vikings 1 and 2	Robot landers on Mars
1981	Columbia	First space shuttle
1981	Voyager 2	Robot space probe passes Saturn
1986	MIR	Space station built from modules
1993	Mars observer	Space probe sent to orbit Mars
1997	Pathfinder	Robot lander on Mars

GLOSSARY

astronomer
a scientist who studies the stars and planets

booster rocket
a small rocket attached to a larger rocket to give extra power at take off

dock
to join two spacecraft or parts of a space station together in space

friction
the force of one thing rubbing against another thing

gravity
a force which pulls things towards the Earth

launch pad
the flat area from which a rocket is launched into space

orbit
the curved path which a planet, moon or satellite follows as it circles around a star or planet

rocket
a tube filled with fuel which burns to thrust the rocket and its cargo away from the ground

satellite
an object such as a spacecraft or television satellite which is in orbit around a planet

shuttle
a spacecraft which can take off, orbit the Earth, land, and be used again

space probe
a robot spacecraft sent to explore other planets

space station
a home and workplace built in space for astronauts to use

spacesuit
the special suit with a helmet that astronauts must wear to survive in space

INDEX